Richard Chenevix Trench

Shipwrecks of Faith

Three Sermons Preached before the University of Cambridge

Richard Chenevix Trench

Shipwrecks of Faith
Three Sermons Preached before the University of Cambridge

ISBN/EAN: 9783744745932

Printed in Europe, USA, Canada, Australia, Japan

Cover: Foto ©Lupo / pixelio.de

More available books at **www.hansebooks.com**

SHIPWRECKS OF FAITH

THREE SERMONS

Preached before the University of Cambridge

IN MAY, 1867

BY

RICHARD CHENEVIX TRENCH, D.D.

ARCHBISHOP

LONDON

KEGAN PAUL, TRENCH, & CO., 1 PATERNOSTER SQUARE

1886

CONTENTS.

SERMON I.

BALAAM.

B

Holding faith, and a good conscience ; which some having put away concerning faith have made shipwreck.

THE first lesson for the service of last Sunday afternoon, and again that for the service of this morning, are wholly occupied with the history of Balaam. They tell us, with one or two important exceptions, all which we know concerning a man, who made one of those signal and disastrous shipwrecks of faith whereof St. Paul in my text has spoken. It has seemed to me that I might not altogether unprofitably use the opportunities afforded to me here, if I were to comment a little to-day on the circumstances of his fall; and then, following up the line of thought which this

consideration will very naturally have suggested, invite you, on the two other Sundays
on which I may hope to have again the privi-
lege of standing here, to contemplate two
others, who are described to us in Scripture as
having made concerning faith the same shipwreck which he made ; or, to use another
image, who are set forth to us there as
beacon-lights, not such as have been kindled
to beckon and to guide into deep waters and
safe harbours, but rather to warn us off from
perilous reefs and quicksands, which have been
the destruction of many, and which might
only too easily be ours.

Doubtless there are many other very
mournful lives in Scripture, besides the three
of which I propose to treat. The Bible would
not be the book *of* men and *for* men were it
otherwise, seeing how many lives inexpressibly
mournful there have been and are in this
actual world—lives to which is attached exactly the same kind of mournfulness which
cleaves to theirs—the lives, I mean, of men

who, called to high things, have yet chosen low; who, called to a crown, have let others take that crown; to a kingdom, and to places there which were nearest the throne, have yet forfeited their places in that kingdom altogether. Such a life, for example, is that of Esau, who, for a mess of pottage, for one morsel of meat, sold his birthright, bartered away an inheritance which was his. Such another is that of Jeroboam, for whom God would have built a sure house, as He built for David, if only he had proved faithful as David proved.[1] A sadness of the same sort rests upon the life of Demas, to whom a share in Paul's crown as well as in Paul's cross was brought so near; but who, loving this present world, preferred to cast in his lot, and to take his doom, with that world which he loved.

At the same time these attain not to the first three. And the three whom I have selected—Balaam the prophet, but the prophet outside the Covenant; Saul, the king

---

[1] 1 Kings, xi. 38.

under the old dispensation; and Judas Iscariot,
the apostle under the new; these three, first
who were also last, present themselves as
in some sort the mournfullest of all, for the
greatness of their vocation, and their disastrous falling short of the same, for the
utter defeat of their lives, for the shipwreck
of everything which they made. And here let
me note that assuredly it was not for nothing
that St. Paul employed such a word as this.
A shipwreck involves for the most part a
perishing, and that without salvage, of all
which had been committed to the ill-fated
bark; and in this way sets forth to us, better
than any other word would have done, a loss
which we have no choice but to consider as
irremediable and total.

The main outlines of the history of Balaam,
and of the events which led to his appearance
on the scene of sacred story, these I have a
right to assume familiar to all whom I ad-
dress. The conquering advance of the armies

of Israel toward the land of their promised possession, the fear of them which spread ever wider and wider among the nations round about—a fear so vigorously expressed in the words of the king of Moab: 'Now shall this company lick up all that are round about us, as the ox licketh up the grass of the field'—the sense on the part of their adversaries, that mere carnal weapons would be wielded against them in vain; the resolution of the king of Moab to summon the famous soothsayer and prophet from the river Euphrates, 'out of the mountains of the east,' that he might come and curse these invaders, and so rob them of that favour of heaven which had made them hitherto invincible,—all this is sufficiently known to us all.

But what was Balaam, this seer from the further east? Was he a prophet indeed, one by whom God had spoken in time past, as it is certain that He spoke by him now? or had he been hitherto merely a dealer in charms

and incantations, and, in so far as he claimed
any direct intercourse with the God of Israel,
a deceiver and a false prophet? The question has been often put, and variously an-
swered. I am persuaded that any answer
which, without reserve, exalts him into the
rank of the prophets of the true God, but
also that any which absolutely and without
qualification denies him a place among these,
will alike fail to meet and satisfy all the facts
of the case ; that in neither of these extremes
is the truth to be found.

Had Balaam been, as some would persuade
us, a mere impostor in times past, a pretender
to an intercourse with God which he never
enjoyed, to the possession of spiritual powers
which stood wholly aloof from him, he would
have occupied no higher moral level than the
rain-maker of a Caffre village, or the medi-
cine-man of some Red Indian tribe. But,
not to urge objections which reach deeper,
Scripture is far too chary of its precious
spaces to expend them upon persons with no

higher moral or spiritual significance than these. Balaam, the son of Beor, offers to us a far more complex problem, stands upon another footing altogether. There can be no doubt that he had been already used of God to utter truths of his kingdom; and here is the explanation of a fact which the king of Moab had not failed to note: ' He whom thou blessest is blessed, and he whom thou cursest is cursed.' [1] This near relation to Jehovah on the part of one outside of the chosen family is perfectly intelligible, if we keep in mind that the strict line of demarcation separating the elect nation from all the other nations of the earth was only just at this moment being drawn. After the full founding of the Jewish theocracy a Melchisedek, or even a Balaam, would have been impossible ; they would have been irreconcilable with that peculiar relation to one people into which God, for the times preceding the Incarnation, had entered. And standing thus, as

---

[1] Num. xxii. 6.

Balaam did, outside of the Covenant, it was possible for him to occupy a moral border-land, in which light and darkness, a true though partial insight into the character of God, and at the same time trust in superstitious enchantments, dwelt side by side with one another. For one occupying a spiritual position such as his there would have been no room in Israel, where, under a clearer dispensation, light and darkness, good and evil, were drawn severally into their opposite camps ; but only in that heathen world, for which at that time the sun of original revelation had not wholly set, however the darkness was now fast settling over all.

We should err too, and take a false estimate of his character, if we conceived of him in the chapters which we have been reading to-day, as a mere mouthpiece of prophecies, which, even at the very moment of uttering, he would fain have withholden if he might ; or would have been still better pleased to change from blessings into curses. He too is borne away, at least for the time, by the grandeur of the announcements which he is making, by the glimpses vouchsafed to him to see and to proclaim, of the glory which shall be revealed. There is that in him which reaches out with a true, although too transient, yearning after the coming triumphs of the people and kingdom of God.

Not then a mere wizard, as little a false prophet, compelled on this one occasion by an overmastering might to be a true one, there were yet in Balaam elements of falsehood only too many. His insight into the character of God, if true in part, was in part also heathenish and false. It could not be otherwise. Not to speak of his position, external to the Covenant, he had further failed to hold the mystery of the faith in a pure conscience; he had given way to sordid temptations; he has allowed covetous and worldly desires, a rank undergrowth of weeds, to spring up in his soul, side by side with what God may have planted there. That sin of covetousness,

which by a strange irony has proved in all
ages the sin most easily besetting those who
are brought into most direct contact with
things spiritual, namely the prophet and the
priest, had done its work only too effectually in
him.   He might move among heavenly things,
but they were earthly things which he minded
the most.   He was one—it is the testimony
of Scripture—' having his heart exercised with
covetous practices.'   Still, though in the end
he was not saved, through putting away faith
and a good conscience, he made fatal shipwreck at the last, we are bound to believe
that, at the time when he first appears before
us, he was saveable.   He was not then, as he
proved in the end, ' to every good thing re-
probate.'   All God's dealings with him would
else have had no meaning; even as his
history would offer comparatively little instruction for us.

   To such a man the messengers of the king
of Moab, bearing in their hands the rewards
of divination, as the sacred historian is careful

to note, have come. He welcomes and enter-
tains them; bids them to tarry for the night;
by that welcoming giving them to understand that he will go with them, and do
what their master requires,—curse, that is, the
people of God,—if only he may obtain permission for this. Here was the beginning of
his fall. He knew that he ought not to go;
but they came to him with those rich and
royal gifts in their hands; and he could not
make up his mind at once to renounce the
hope of these, even if he must resign them at
the last. He will dally a little with the
temptation; look at it for a while on its
pleasant side; see if he cannot by some
means or other reconcile it with his conscience, or yield to it without wounding his
conscience overmuch; for Balaam is at this
time in the main a conscientious man. He
will act, brethren, exactly as we act, when we
give any sort of allowance to that which, however pleasant, ought to have been put from
us at once; contemplate it on the side upon

which it flatters our appetite, and promises
pleasure; when we cast about for devices by
which we may give it room without utterly
ruining our standing before God; when we do
this, instead of regarding it from the first in
its sinfulness and its danger, and as that
which is no more to be played with than the
fire, no more to be taken to the bosom than
a poisonous adder could be safely cherished
there.

And yet, though he has dangerously dallied
with his temptation, he has not on this first
occasion fallen under it. There is so much
fear of God in the prophet, that the express
prohibition, 'Thou shalt not go with them,'
is enough; while yet his words of apology,
'The Lord refuseth to give me leave to go
with you,' show only too plainly where his
heart and his heart's affections are; that he
'loves the wages of unrighteousness,' even
though as yet he is not prepared at all costs
to grasp and make them his own. For this
time he has triumphed, or has seemed to

triumph; but ah! brethren, how little profit
there is in overcoming a first temptation, if
we succumb to a second or a third; if all
the while there are secret correspondencies
between us and the sin which we put back
from us, inviting renewed assaults on the part
of our tempter. And is it not sometimes
with us too much as it was with this man,
that we are only waiting to be tempted
enough, that we love a strong temptation,
one which, beaten back a little, presently
returns in greater strength, because it seems
to afford an excuse, nay, almost a justifica-
tion, for our yielding? Such secret correspondencies with sin were here; and the king
of Moab—he was the tempter here, although
there was a mightier Tempter behind—quite
understood the man with whom he had to
deal. In that 'No' of his he could detect a
lurking 'Yes;' could read plainly, 'Yes, if I
dared;' and, instead of accepting that refusal
as final, he sends to him more and more
honourable messengers than before, by this

embassage flattering his pride; and these with larger promises on their lips, so meeting the the covetous desires of his heart.

A second time tempted, it might almost seem as though he were about a second time to overcome. His refusal now is even more emphatic than at the first : ' If Balak would give me his house full of silver and gold, I cannot go beyond the word of the Lord my God, to do less or more ; '—more emphatic, but only as men shroud a failing resolution of heart, by putting additional strength in their words. It is lip-service, lip-homage all. Real conformity with the will of God there is none; else he would have owned that he had gotten his instructions already, and had nothing to do now but to obey them. But instead of this, instead of dismissing the messengers at once, he bids them tarry for the night, that he may know what the Lord will say unto him more. Very perilous it is to ask oracles from God in such a spirit as this; very fatal it proved to him; for now it is told him, ' If

the men come to call thee, rise up and go
with them;' as though God had said, 'Thy
heart is set on this journey; go, therefore, if
thou wilt. I will not stand any longer in the
way of thy desire.' Oh dreadful judgment
of our God, when He permits in anger what
He had long refused in love; when He says
concerning the sinner, 'If thou art so mad
upon thine idols, thou shalt even be filled with
them and with thine own ways. If nothing
will satisfy thy lust but the quails, thou shalt
even surfeit upon them, till they become
loathsome to thee, or till thou perish while the
meat is yet in thy mouth. If thou prayest
that I depart out of thy coasts, I will even
grant thy prayer, and depart, carrying away
with me all those treasures of my grace with
which I had thought to make thee rich for
ever.' Oh dreadful judgment of our God, to
have our way made plain before us, when that
way itself is a crooked one, and leading to
those dark mountains on which men stumble
and fall, and are for ever broken. And this

was the judgment of the prophet now, who
greedily snatched at a permission, the character of which, as one taught of God, he should
have better understood.

But although God's anger is kindled against
him because he went, He does not, therefore,
forsake him. Balaam may perish, if he be
in love with death, and resolved that his covenant with it shall not be broken; but he shall
not perish without at least one more effort to
save him. The Angel of the Lord stands in
the strait and narrow path (it was a broad
way enough in another sense), to stay him.
But the prophet's eye was utterly darkened.
Covetousness, love of this world, passionate
eagerness for its honours and rewards, had so
dimmed and darkened that spiritual eye by
which he should have discerned this heavenly
appearance, this Messenger of the Divine
anger and the Divine love, that he could see
nothing; while, strange reversal of parts! that
spiritual vision, which is thus invisible to him
who by his very office was a *Seer*, is visible to

the natural brute beast, which, by the very constitution of its nature, seemed absolutely and for ever excluded from every vision of the kind. So was rebuked, although but for a moment, the madness of the prophet; who would else have rushed even then upon destruction, and fallen beneath the Angel's sword.

It needs not for me to remind you with what passionate displeasure he encountered these checks and obstacles so graciously placed in his way. Only I would ask you, my brethren, has our God in his grace never in like manner withstood us, when our way was perverse before Him; thwarted us in schemes of which we only perceive the full sinfulness now; mercifully hedged up our ways with thorns, that we could not find our paths,—our paths, which were not his? and yet, instead of saying as David said to Abigail when she hindered him from a deed of blood, 'Blessed be the Lord God which sent thee this day to meet me,' we have fretted at this opposition, perhaps raged against it, perhaps in our folly have overborne it; as mad upon our idols as was ever Balaam upon his, and almost as much in love with our own ruin as he was with his?

But the end is not yet. All obstacles disastrously surmounted, he has arrived at length at the court of the king of Moab, and is, as we cannot doubt, as indeed we are expressly told, made much of there; the king himself going to receive him at the very borders of his land, and only reproaching him that he had not come before, to claim the honours and rewards which were waiting for him. We might have expected this; for, indeed, none are made more of, none are more fawned on and flattered, at least for a little while, than spiritual men when they stoop to serve the purposes of the world; lending, as they seem to do, a consecration of heaven to the schemes of earth, wielding the powers of the world to come in the interests of the children of this world. None, I say, are more flattered and fawned on for a season; although,

when once they have profaned and made
common themselves, their gifts, and their
office, none are cast off with intenser scorn
and loathing and contempt; the world reject-
ing them as the sea presently rejects and
vomits back the corpses which itself has swal-
lowed up. However unjust the executors of
the sentence, the sentence itself is a just one.
The prophet that telleth lies, let him be the
tail; and saltless salt is most fitly cast out and
trodden under foot, not of God, but of men.
But this day of scorn and contempt has not
yet arrived for Balaam. It must first be seen
to what present service he may be turned.
Yet they who have summoned obtain not from
him the service which they had hoped. God
had told him, when he went at their bidding,
' The word which I shall say unto thee, that
shalt thou do;' and so it proves; for, indeed,
all men serve Him; some willingly, and find
in that service a blessing and a reward; some
unwillingly, who, missing the blessing altogether, do not the less serve Him, the bad

working together with the good for the fulfilling of his designs, for the setting forward of
his kingdom; even as in Jewish legend the
wicked spirits are compelled by Solomon
to assist in rearing the temple of the true
God.

You heard in the chapters of this morning
of the word which the Lord put into Balaam's
mouth, of the blessings instead of curses
which, willing or unwilling, he uttered; and
of all which in ecstatic vision it was given
him to behold, even 'the giant forms of em-
pire on their way to ruin;' and all to make
room, as the world-kingdoms must, for that
kingdom which ruleth over all, and for Him
who in that kingdom is the King: 'There
shall come a Star out of Jacob, and a Sceptre
shall rise out of Israel.' Glorious words,
which yet that prophet could not utter without this significant addition, 'I shall see
Him, but not now; I shall behold Him, but
not nigh.' So saying, he may indeed have
meant no more than that the rising of that

Star, the budding of that Sceptre, were yet afar off—should not be till those ' latter days,' which constitute the limiting horizon for the prophets of an earlier time. And yet, whether he may have intended it or no, what another sadder truth the words had for him. For the good things which he ministered to others he ministered them not to himself; and such, therefore, was the only seeing which he should ever share. That Star, even ' the bright and the Morning Star,' he should never walk in its light; it should never gild or gladden him with its beams. That Sceptre, he should never know it as a golden Sceptre stretched out to him in love, that he might touch it, and that, touching, he might live ; but only as a rod of anger, which should break him utterly in pieces. Ah, brethren, we who have been set to announce to others a day-star already risen, even Christ the Lord,—a sceptre of grace which the Great King even now stretches out in pardoning love to all who draw nigh to Him in faith, and you who shall hereafter be heralds to announce the same, let us all accept the warning which in these words is for us involved. Knowledge without love; insight, at least of one kind, into heavenly mysteries, with a heart all the while cleaving to earth and the earth's dross; a ministry to others of good things in which we have no part nor portion ourselves, are we content that this should be ours? Can we imagine a more miserable defeat than this, of all for which our life was lent, and we called to our high office, and endowed with special gifts and powers for its fulfilling, and for the saving at once of others and also of ourselves?

And now the end is at hand. There is but one step more in that way downward, which the unhappy and guilty prophet has been treading so long. Driven with disgrace and dishonour from the presence of him at whose bidding he had undertaken this ill-omened journey, having offended God without pleasing men, like so many who forfeit heaven and

yet fail to win earth, who letting go the substance, snatch at the shadow, and miss
shadow and substance alike, he makes one
last and desperate effort to obtain the favour
and the rewards which he sees escaping from
his hands; and he, the man *to* whom, and *by*
whom, God had spoken, who saw the vision
of the Almighty, whose eyes God has opened,
is the author of the devilish suggestion that
the children of Israel should be seduced to
uncleanness, so robbed of their righteousness;
and thus, when there *is* iniquity in Jacob, and
perverseness in Israel, lie open, being stripped
of their divine armour, as an easy prey to the
enemies whom else they would have defied.
The Antichrist of the desert history, for this
devilish device of his has proclaimed him to
be nothing less, it is no wonder that a little
later he is entangled in their doom with
whom he has made common cause against
God; and that, when the Midianites perish
beneath the sword of Joshua, he should perish
with them. There is something very signi-

ficant in the brief parenthetic notice which
records his doom : ' And Balaam, the son of
Beor, they slew with the sword.'

And this is the man, in arms against Israel
and Israel's God, thus rushing on the bosses
of the shield of the Almighty, to be utterly
broken there, who had exclaimed a little while
before, ' Surely there is no enchantment
against Jacob; neither is there any divination against Israel. The Lord his God is
with him, and the shout of a king is among
them.' This is the man, so miserably ending,
who had exclaimed, ' Let me die the death
of the righteous, and let my last end be like
his ; ' and who had meant what he said ; who,
for the moment at least, had seen the blessed-
ness of such an end, and had desired that
such might be his own. Very unlike the
ending of the righteous his end has proved.
And yet, brethren, what but some such issue
was possible for the life of one, to whom
so much had been committed, and who
had finished with turning against God all

which by God had been thus committed
to him?

> 'Alas! yet wherefore mourn? The law
> Is holier than a sage's prayer;
> The godlike power bestowed on men
> Demands of them a godlike care.
> And noblest gifts, if basely used,
> Will sternliest avenge the wrong;
> And grind with slavish pangs the slave
> Whom once they made divinely strong.'

They will do this; or they will drive him
into desperate conflict with their Author and
their Giver, to perish, as did Balaam at the
last, an enemy of all righteousness, an open
fighter against the God of all holiness and
goodness and truth.

SERMON II.

SAUL.

Holding faith, and a good conscience; which some having put away concerning faith have made shipwreck.

MANY have loved to trace the points of resemblance between the two Sauls of Scripture, the two illustrious Benjamites, in whom all which was worst and all which was best in that fierce and daring tribe, so capable of evil, and so capable of good, came to a head : the one belonging to the Old Covenant, the other to the New. These points of resemblance are not merely superficial and external. There is something more than name and tribe which is common to them both. The second Saul for a while followed only too faithfully in the footsteps of the first. If the one persecuted

David, the other,—with an energy of hate
which did not fall short of his, — David's
greater Son. Presently, however, their lives
divide, and one is the Saul of reprobation, the
other, not being disobedient to the heavenly
voices, the Saul of election; although he
too, in the prompt audacities of his apostolic
career, does not allow us to forget, as we know
that he did not himself forget, of what tribe
he was, of that tribe of Benjamin, which pro-
duced its noblest representative in him.

But of Saul, who was also Paul, I speak
not to-day; rather of that other Saul, who
abode in his old nature to the end; who,
anointed captain of the Lord's inheritance,
and endowed from on high with gifts for an
office of so surpassing a dignity, did yet after
a while miserably forget *from* whom he held,
and *for* whom he wielded, all; who, refusing
to follow on to know the Lord, let go that
good thing which had been committed to
him; and not this only, for he who has once
tasted of the powers of the world to come, can

never be, for good or for evil, merely what he was before, but made in the end such a ship-wreck of faith and a good conscience as leaves his story among the saddest which Scripture anywhere contains. It is this story which, in the carrying out of a purpose which I indi-cated last Sunday, will furnish my subject for to-day. The fact of the remarkable detail in which the events of Saul's life are reported to us would itself be a strong presumption that his story was one which it concerned us much that we should be intimately acquainted with; while a closer study abundantly bears out and justifies this presumption. Let me as-sume, then, such a familiarity to be already yours, and proceed to draw from his story some of those lessons of instruction and warn-ing which it is so capable of yielding.

I will ask you to notice first—for this is most important—the singular elements of nobleness which are to be traced in his na-tural character; so that his moral stature did not altogether belie the stateliness of his outward frame. Let me briefly remind you of some of those nobler features which we can have scarcely failed to recognize in him. There is nothing which so often oversets the whole balance of a mind, which brings out at once faults unsuspected before, as a sudden and abrupt elevation from a very low to a very high position. Now, there has been seldom a more abrupt elevation than was Saul's. But he gives no token, at all events at the outset of his career, that it has wrought this mischief in him. The Lord's anointed, Israel's king, he bides his time, returns with a true simplicity to humblest offices in his father's house.[1] He would gladly, and that out of a genuine modesty, hide and withdraw himself from the people's choice.[2] Slights and offences done to himself he magnanimously overlooks; absolutely refuses to punish the authors of these, when busy sycophants would prompt and urge him to a bloody revenge.[3]

---

[1] 1 Sam. xi. 5.   [2] 1 Sam. x. 21, 22.
[3] 1 Sam. x. 27; xi. 13.

Neither are there wanting in him genuine traits of that, which indeed is as old as any human nobleness, but which in modern times we have learned to call the spirit of chivalry; he will venture his life far for the people whom he rules, as one who has rightly understood that foremost in place and in honour means also foremost in peril and in toil; that he who has accepted the one pre-eminence has implicitly also accepted the other.[1] Saul is clear from every charge of that sin which left the darkest blot upon David's life; seems very sparingly to have allowed himself that license which almost all Oriental monarchs, alike in old times and in new, have so largely claimed. There was in him, as we cannot refuse to acknowledge, a true capacity for loving. Of David, we are told, he 'loved him greatly;'[2] however that love of his was afterwards, under the influence of a jealous envy, transformed into hate.

And then, further, he is very far from

[1] 1 Sam. xi. 6-11.   [2] 1 Sam. xvi. 21.

absolutely repelling all impressions from a higher world. Saul too, though to the wonder of many, is 'among the prophets;'[1] and prophesies with them. God, we are told, 'gave him another heart;' 'he was turned into another man,'[2] though, alas! too soon returning to the old man and to the old nature again.

And even at his worst, when he has given place to the devil, to those powers from beneath which do battle in every human heart against the powers from above, what glimpses of a better mind from time to time reappear. The old affection revives for an instant: 'Is this thy voice, my son David?' He can understand magnanimity, and for the moment is prepared to reply to it with the like.[3] The deep discords of his spirit are not incapable of being subdued into harmonies, as sweet bells jangled and out of tune, which for an instant, though, alas! but for an in-

---

[1] 1 Sam. x. 11.; xix. 24.   [2] 1 Sam. x. 6, 9.
[3] 1 Sam. xxiv. 16; xxvi. 17.

stant, recover their sweetness. And most
noticeable of all, the love which he could feel
he could also inspire. For one altogether
unworthy to be loved, Samuel would have
never interceded, would have never mourned,
as he interceded and mourned for Saul; per-
sisting in this until God, almost in displeasure
that his will was not in more perfect conformity with the Divine will, demanded,
'How long wilt thou mourn for Saul?'[1]
When too David sang of him and of Jona-
than, 'They were lovely and pleasant in their
lives,' this was not an example of that flattery
in which men too often allow themselves concerning the dead, but did express what one
who had known him, as almost none other
could have known, who had suffered from
him nearly all which one man could suffer
from another, yet felt to be the truth; not,
indeed, all the truth, but truth notwithstand-
ing. If, then, there was a shipwreck here (as
who can deny it?) they were not paltry wares,

[1] 1 Sam. xv. 35; xvi. 1.

but treasures of great price, which went down into the great deep.

Time would not permit, nay, it would defeat the objects of a discourse, were I to attempt to follow, step by step, the course of the trial of Saul, the manner in which a fair dawn was presently darkened and overcast. In the necessity of things we must foreshorten, deal with results, rapidly allude to events on which we cannot dwell. I will thus do no more than refer to the impatience and unbelief which led him to offer a sacrifice contrary to the express command of God by the mouth of the prophet Samuel.[1] As little need I remind you of another sin and a graver, which followed on the back of this, namely, the flying on the spoil, which he had been commanded utterly to destroy ; or of that whole determination, which after a while made itself only too evident upon his part, to use for his own glory, and according to his own pleasure, what had

[1] 1 Sam. xiii. 8–14.

been lent him for God's glory, and for the fulfilling of the good pleasure of his will; until at length, having been weighed in the balances, and found wanting, convinced of stubbornness, obstinacy, and rebellion, the terrible sentence was pronounced against him : ' Because thou hast rejected the word of the Lord, He hath also rejected thee from being king.' [1] On all this it will be impossible to dwell in detail.

On one matter, however, I will dwell a little, as the sum total of the impression which the study of the life of Saul up to this, which may be called the crisis of it, must, I think, leave upon the minds of us all. To my mind, at least, there is no history which, as we read it, brings home to us a stronger sense, perhaps none so strong a sense, of this life which each one of us is living, as a life of probation ; no history which makes us so vividly to realize the fact, that God takes men and puts them in certain conditions to try them; to

[1] 1 Sam. xv. 23.

see how they will bear themselves under these
conditions, how far they will profit by the
opportunities for good, resist the solicitations
to evil which these will inevitably offer to
them. Now, we all admit in words the fact
that life is a probation ; to a certain extent,
we even realize the fact about others, about
the historical personages of Scripture, about
persons suddenly raised to vast wealth, or put
into the possession of almost unlimited power ;
or who, having enjoyed these, are at a stroke
deprived of them. But we realize the fact
very faintly, if at all, about ourselves.

The circumstances which surround us seem
to differ so slightly from those which surround
any other, they appear to so large an extent the result of chance, they have become
to us, after a little while, so much matters of
course, that the disciplinary, probationary
character of them nearly or altogether escapes
us. And yet He who holds our lives in the
hollow of his hand is as surely proving us by
these, as He was proving Saul by that king-

dom to which He raised him. We are each
one of us upon our trial as certainly as he
was upon his.

For instance, the enormous increase in freedom of action which the beginning of college
life brings with it; the new and far more irre-
sponsible command of time, of money, on the
part of one hitherto under tutors and gover-
nors, can any one on whom this has come,
refuse to acknowledge that he is being tried
by it? The fact that a young man who
chooses to be idle at a University, may be
almost as idle as he pleases—for the little of
deceitful eye-service which may be extorted
from one unwilling to render more, does not
materially alter the fact, or affect my statement—is not this an enormous and a most
perilous trial? Is it not being seen what you
will make of this liberty? how far you can
bear, whether you will abuse it? That the
same is happening to multitudes round you,
this surely does not alter the nature of the fact.

We return to his history who has suggested

these observations. Many a terrible word has been uttered against a sinful man, as against Ahab—or a sinful nation, as against the Ninevites—which yet has been suspended or reversed, when these have humbled themselves under the mighty and uplifted hand of God; and, despite of that sentence, 'The Lord hath rejected thee,' who knows how far this might have been the case with Saul, if only that humbling of himself had been found in him? But this is exactly what was wanting through his whole career. No feature is more striking in his history, none serves more to explain that history, than the entire absence of this. When accused by Samuel, he puts himself instantly on the defensive; finds cloaks, excuses, justifications of his sin, lays the fault of it upon others.[1] If he confess that sin, it is, as our ancestors were wont to call it, 'from the teeth outward,' never from a true penitent heart. If Samuel will honour him before the people, and so it shall not be evident to all

---

[1] 1 Sam. xv. 20, 21.

that God has ceased to honour him—this is
the sum of his desires.[1]   And, therefore, the
sentence stands fast; and he walks the re-
mainder of his course,—and it was a long one,
for he was king for some forty years,—a man
rejected and forbid.   No wonder that all the
worse lines of his character deepen and darken,
that the Spirit of the Lord departs from him,
and an evil spirit troubles him.[2]   He gives
place to the devil more and more; jealousy
ripens into a murderous hate;[3] he is visited
by accesses of madness, and falls into ever
deeper confusions of the inner spirit and the
outer life.

There are few more difficult questions, in
the case of minds utterly distempered and
disordered as his was, than to determine
where sin, or moral disease, has ended, and
madness, or mental disease, has begun.   There
is an obscure and mysterious border-land,
where these two seem inextricably mingled,
acting and reacting the one upon the other.

[1] 1 Sam. xv. 30.   [2] 1 Sam. xvi. 14.   [3] 1 Sam. xix. 1.

Thus, who can doubt that more than one of
those monsters of lust and cruelty who occupied the throne of imperial Rome had passed,
or had nearly passed, out of the number of
responsible beings, before their own or some
assassin's dagger rid the world of their presence ? And yet who does not at the same
time feel, that though they may not have
been guilty for what they wrought in that
frenzy of their minds, this only throws back
their guilt a single stage, seeing that it was
through lavish indulgence in allowed sin that
all this evil had come upon them. With only
these remarks I leave this part of the life of
Saul, not attempting to determine how far it
had thus fared with him ; how far an habitual
self-command might have averted, how far
the opposite to this drew upon him, those
visitations of moody madness, in which he
attempted the life, now of David, and now of
his own son. I leave all this, for I must
hasten to the concluding scene of his career.

You know the end, and all which led up to

the end ; how he, who had long grieved the
Holy Spirit of God, showed at last that he
had quenched it ; for only so could he have
committed that sin against light and knowledge, that act of open apostasy from the
God of Israel, which fills up the measure of
his long rebellion against Him. Saul will
summon by an evil magic—for such might
was supposed by the heathen world to lie in
charms and incantations, and there is a
heathenish element in him, as in every man,
and one which has now the upper hand—he
will fain summon, by aid of these, the dead
from their graves, and win from the world
of darkness and of death that knowledge
which the world of light and of life refuses to
impart to him. This consulting with the
witch of Endor on the part of Israel's anointed
king was probably as nearly the sin against
the Holy Ghost as it was possible for one
under the Old Covenant, and before the day
of Pentecost, to commit.

The scene is one which, in its own especial

kind of grandeur and of terror, is unique in
Scripture. Only let me observe that all, or
nearly all, of its dread significance is lost, and
it sinks down to a level with those juggling
tricks which are the dishonour of the present
age by the wide credit they have obtained, so
long as we regard the apparition of Samuel
as an imposture palmed upon the king by
the woman who professed to raise him. As
little may we regard it as a piece of devilish
magic, the prince of lies by himself, or by one
of his inferior ministers, personating the dead
prophet, and speaking in his name. This
apparition of the dead Samuel in answer to
these enchantments—for it is the prophet
himself who answers—is rather, as it was
long ago remarked, a wonderful fulfilment of
those words of God by the prophet Ezekiel,
'Every one of the house of Israel which
separateth himself from Me, and setteth up
his idols in his heart, and putteth the stumbling-block of his iniquity before his face, and
cometh to a prophet to enquire of him con-

cerning Me, I the Lord will answer him by Myself' (xiv. 7). He did thus answer Saul, who had put the stumbling-block of his iniquity before his face, and had so come to enquire of the Lord, by Himself; and none was more amazed at the success of her necromancies than the sorceress herself.

But of all this we cannot here speak in particular. Only I am sure you will agree with me, that all human art would fail to portray, that all human history has failed to record, a despair deeper or more tragic than his, who, having forsaken God and being of God forsaken, is now seeking to move hell, since heaven is inexorable to him; and, infinitely guilty as he is, assuredly there is something unutterably pathetic in that yearning of the disanointed king, now in his utter desolation to change words once more with the friend and counsellor of his youth; and, if he must hear his doom, to hear it from no other lips but his. And was confession more utterly forlorn ever yet extorted from

human lips: 'I am sore distressed; for the
Philistines make war against me, and God is
departed from me, and answereth me no
more, neither by prophets nor by dreams;
therefore I have called thee, that thou may-
est make known unto me what I shall do?'[1]
Then too the answering words of the seer,
'To-morrow shalt thou be with me,' mourn-
fully remind us of another prediction, 'This
day shalt thou be with Me in paradise,'—a
prediction like to this, but how unlike too;
for one was spoken to a penitent, the other to
an impenitent, sinner.

And, indeed, in all this terrible scene the
most terrible fact of all is the total absence
of all penitence on the part of Saul. He was
clear, as I noted just now, of offences which
make some pages in David's history nothing
better than one huge blot. But oh! how
much better it would have been to have
sinned like David, if only he had repented
like David; if a temper resembling at all the

temper which dictated the 51st Psalm had
found place in him. But all this was far
from him. Darkness is closing round him;
anguish has taken hold of him; but the
broken and the contrite heart, there is no
remotest sign or token of this; no reaching
out after the blood of sprinkling. We listen,
but no voice is heard like his who exclaimed,
' Purge me with hyssop, and I shall be clean ;
wash me, and I shall be whiter than snow;'
but dark and defiant and unbelieving, he who
had inspired such high hopes, he who for a
while seemed about to justify them all, goes
forward to meet his doom.

What that doom was we know. That his
sun should set in blood, I count not this of
itself any so dreadful a thing. There are
many lives which have had as bloody a setting
as his had, which have been poured out in
disastrous battle as was his; which yet, as we
contemplate their close, fill us with a solemn
thankfulness and gladness, such as no words
could utter so well as those inexpressibly

E

noble ones in Milton, spoken over a fallen
champion of the faith :—

> ' Nothing is here for tears, nothing to wail,
>   Or knock the breast; nothing but well and fair,
>   And what may quiet us in a death so noble.'

But it was not so here. Over the close of
this life there broods a thick and comfortless
darkness, even the darkness of a night without a star.

A very few practical lessons, by way of
conclusion, for ourselves. At the opening of
my discourse I invited you, my brethren,
to recognize the finer elements which the
character of Saul displays. But I must
beseech you now not to lose sight of the very
significant fact, that all these display themselves at the outset of his career; that they
gradually fade and fail from him—the humility,
the generosity, the disregard of slights offered
to himself, with whatever else of better he may
have owned at the first; pride meanwhile,
and caprice, and jealousy, cruelty, an exces-
sive avenging of himself, and at last an open

contempt and defiance of God, coming in their room; until of all the high qualities which he once owned only the courage, last gift to forsake a man, often abiding when every other has departed, until this only remains. I know not, brethren, whether the world has anything to show at all so mournful as the spectacle which we have here; namely, the gradual breaking down under the wear and tear of the world, under the influence of un-resisted temptations, of a lofty soul; the un-worthy close of a life worthily ·begun—as though some clear and rolling river should lose itself in a sullen and stagnant marsh, instead of bringing in due time the volume of its tributary and ever-waxing waters to the main.

Who is there that would willingly even in thought be judge of his fellow-men? Yet we cannot refuse to note what is visibly pass-ing before our eyes; and as many among us as are old enough to have been able to watch the gradual development of lives, can hardly

have failed to note, on the one side, some who,
giving little promise at the commencement of
their career, have yet afterwards risen into
clearness of purpose, dignity of aim, the
stream of their life at once deepening and
purifying as it ran; while others of much
rarer and ampler gifts, framed in a far richer
prodigality of nature, and this not merely in
respect of intellectual gifts, but of affections
as well, have yet, as the years rolled on,
seemed to lose and let go what once they
had; have contracted their aims, lowered
their standard, narrowed their souls—the
good that was in them has seemed to fade
and fail; it may be some root of bitterness
springing up in them has marred and mis-
chiefed it altogether; till in the end they
creep by obscure and narrow passages to
their graves.

What is the explanation of all this, of the
rising of some, of the falling of others; of
the Jacobs, who, with many and most serious
faults, are yet elevated and exalted into

Israel, princes with God; and of the Esaus, who, not without a certain native generosity, separate themselves off in the end from all which is highest, and truest, and best? The explanation is not far to seek. The relation in which any man stands to God must ultimately determine everything else about him; and when I say to God, I mean to God in Christ, even as there is now no possible standing for any man with God, except in Him: 'No man cometh to the Father but by Me;' 'He that hath the Son, hath life; he that hath not the Son, hath not life.' Jacob, with all those faults of his, wanting as he was in that inborn royalty of spirit, that generosity of nature, so attractive in an Abraham and a David, had yet a side on which he was turned toward God; he could see in vision what Esau could have never seen, namely, the heaven open, and angels ascending and descending by the shining stairs which linked that heaven with the earth he trod; and as his life drew on, he more and more left what was poorer and meaner behind him; he more and more grew into likeness to that higher and heavenly world with which he held habitual communion. But a side turned toward God was exactly that which Esau had not. Good-nature, which he had— and how instructive a word have we here— good-nature is but nature after all; and it left him by the unerring verdict of Scripture, a 'profane person.'[1] Dwell a little, I beseech you again, on that word, as on the Greek of which it is the rendering,—a 'profane person,' —one, that is, without a fane, without a sanctuary in his soul; for whom all things were common, common as the outer court of some temple, which, unfenced and unguarded, is trod and trampled on by the careless foot of every passer-by.

Young men,—if speaking to all, I may yet speak to you in particular,—take, I beseech you, your lesson away with you, even the lesson which the Sauls and Esaus have bequeathed

[1] Heb. xii. 16.

us. Build on no good thing which you find
in yourselves. Humane, generous, high-
minded, brave, you may be; cherishing large
purposes for the welfare of others; willing to
devote yourselves in a spirit of earnest self-
sacrifice to their good. But life is strong—
how strong none can guess till they have tried
—to abate the edge of high resolutions, to
dwarf, to stunt, and, at last, to strangle the
nobler growths of the soul; to lead men to
forget, sometimes, alas! to despise, the loftier
dreams and purer aspirations of their youth.
There is only one pledge for the permanence
of any good thing that is in you—namely, that
you bring it *to* God, and that you receive it
back *from* God, with that higher consecration
which He only can give it; not now any
more a virtue of this world, but a grace of the
kingdom of heaven; and that you bring it to
Him again and again; for indeed all your
fresh springs must be in Him; and they that
wait on Him, they, and they only, renew
their strength—run, and are not weary—walk,

and are not faint; they, and they only, 'bring
forth fruit in old age, to show how true the
Lord is, and that there is no unrighteousness
in Him.' Whatever love of things noble, or
pure, or true, or of good report, He may have
implanted in you, first praise *Him* for this;
and then see that the love of them be wrought
into the very frame and tissue of your souls
and spirits by his Holy Spirit; for assuredly
so, and in no other way, will that love abide
with you to the end.

Sermon III.

JUDAS ISCARIOT.

*Holding faith, and a good conscience ; which
some having put away concerning faith have
made shipwreck.*

IT has been my task in two preceding
discourses to speak of two, a prophet and
a king, who, putting away faith and a good
conscience concerning faith made shipwreck.
A third remains behind—of whom I am this
day to say something—his story the most
tragic of all. For surely if the tragedy of
any man's life consist in the contrast between
what he is and what he might have been,
between depths to which he has fallen and
heights to which he might have risen (and
none, I imagine, will deny this), there was
never doom so tragic as his, who, terrible

contradiction! was at once the apostle and
betrayer of his Lord. For to what had he
been called? what was it that he might
have been? One of the twelve precious
stones on the breast-plate of the everlasting
High Priest; one of the twelve foundations
of the Heavenly Jerusalem, one of the twelve
apostles of the Lamb, even of them that in
the regeneration, in the new heaven and the
new earth, should sit on thrones judging the
twelve tribes of Israel; one whom in all ages
and throughout all the world the Church
should have held in highest honour and thank-
fullest remembrance, as of those who stood
nearest to her Lord when He sojourned
among the children of men. Such he might
have been; and what is he? A name which is
beneath every name, the darkest blot in the
page of human story; and, when we seek to
pierce into the awful darkness beyond, we
only know that One who knows all destinies,
and who measures all dooms, declared of him
what He never in so many words declared of

any other, ' It had been good for that man if
he had not been born.' It is such a shipwreck
of faith and a good conscience as this, which
to-day we have to consider.

It was necessary for me, in my last discourse, to dwell at some length on the many
winning and attractive features which the
character of Saul at one time displayed; to
invite your attention to the outlines of a true
nobleness, traced by the hand of God, which
it was for him to have filled in; but which,
he not caring to do this, were themselves
obliterated at the last. It must be freely
acknowledged that these are wanting in him
with whom we are this day concerned ; or, at
any rate, that there are none such of which
the Scripture had cared to keep record. But
if these are absent, still it is impossible not to
recognize in him features of strength, even
possibilities of greatness, which, as they carried him far in one direction, so, if they had
not been perverted, might have carried him
far in another.

Consider, for example, the infinite self-possession of the man. The more we contemplate this, the more marvellous it must appear. A child of darkness, walking up and down among the children of light, there is nothing in him to betray the secret of that dark world which claims him as its own. At an early period in their ministry his fellow apostles knew that they were twelve whom Christ had chosen, and that one of them was a devil;[1] and yet no special suspicion seems ever to have lighted upon him. And when, as the time drew near, their Lord declared more plainly yet, 'One of you shall betray Me,' the question which rose up in the heart of each, which found utterance from the lips of each, was not, 'Is it he?' but, 'Is it I?' To the very last he maintained his position and a certain moral ascendancy among them. At the supper in Bethany, so prevailing is the influence which he exerts over other disciples, that he is able to draw some of

[1] John vi. 70.

these into a common indignation with himself
at those prodigalities of love which Mary
lavished with grateful hand and heart upon
her Lord.[1] Nay, when he went out from the
Paschal Supper to set the last seal to his
crime, two only knew, and they because their
Lord had indicated to them as much, on
what an errand he was bound : the others did
not so much as guess it.[2] How marvellous a
self-command does all this imply—that he
should never have winced under those pier-
cing but loving words with which his Lord
sought to win him back from his sin; never
by one incautious word, or look, or gesture,
betrayed to those with whom he was living in
intercourse the most familiar, the world of
evil thoughts and imaginations which was
harbouring within him.

So too, when it comes to the last, when he
shall deliver to wicked men Him with whom
he had walked in the house of God as friends,

---

[1] Matt. xxvi. 8 ; John xii. 4, 5.
[2] John xiii. 28, 29.

he does not shrink from openly claiming his share in the treachery. Another, having put the officers of the High Priest on the right track, might himself have lurked behind, and left them to complete the work for themselves. Not so he. You remember the words of St. John—words of wonder upon his part, as I take them to be: 'And Judas also, which betrayed Him, stood with them.' Nor is this all; but, rising to the full height of the wickedness which he is accomplishing, with a kiss, the token of innermost mutual affection, he consummates that act of deadliest hate which the world has ever seen, herein calling out the marvel even of that Lord, who had known him so long and so well, and who supposed that He had sounded all the depths of his sin: 'Betrayest thou the Son of man with a kiss?'

Then, too, a meaner criminal, one of the abjects of the earth, would have clutched the miserable dole which he had earned, would have sought to make the most of those relations which a common guilt had established between himself and the Pharisees ; or, if they had not permitted this, would have been their sycophant and slave, ready to do for them all vilest drudging work to the end. But this man, if he is not capable of repentance, is at all events capable of the dread caricature of repentance, namely, of remorse. He can look his sin in the face; he can call it by its right name, ' I have betrayed the innocent blood ;' he can upbraid to their faces the very chiefs of his people, with a fierce energy forcing himself into the presence of these, and hurling the price of blood, the accursed thing, into the sanctuary itself, and then rushing to that fearful consummation of all, whereof a word presently must be spoken.

All those schemes, so elaborately devised, for reducing the guilt of Judas to a minimum, as, for instance, that he had grown impatient of the Lord's hesitations and delays, and only wished to force Him to declare Himself, and to take the kingdom which was his, and

never contemplated the actual issue, or that
Christ would not at once triumph over his
enemies,—all these may be dismissed as
nothing worth. However ingenious, there is
no foundation for them whatever in the sacred
story; there is much there irreconcilable with
them. Judas Iscariot must remain for us
'the son of perdition,' which the Scripture
names him. But with all this it is no ordinary sinner who stands here before us; as
indeed that very phrase, 'the son of perdition,' common to him and to the Man of
Sin, the Antichrist of the latter days, and not
applied to any other, would itself sufficiently
indicate; not to say that any other, any one
of the more ordinary sinners of the world,
would have failed to reach to the colossal
height of his crime.

There is much about this fallen apostle
which must always remain more or less
obscure to us. Little of what was working
in that dark and self-contained soul was
suffered to escape. We can but piece and

put together the fragmentary notices which Scripture furnishes, and attempt to frame from them, as best we may, some not inconsistent whole. There is the difficulty, first, why he should have offered himself to the service of the Lord; and, secondly, why the Lord, who knew what was in man, should have accepted the service which he offered.

And, first, what was it that drew him into that service at all? That the motives were from the beginning utterly mean and sordid and unworthy, it is impossible for us to believe: one moved by no other must have been put back and rejected at once. No doubt he shared with his fellow apostles in the great hopes of a kingdom, of that kingdom which David's Son and Israel's King should establish. But that which fatally differenced between him and them was this,—they, in the presence and under the teaching of their Lord, suffered these expectations to be transformed and transfigured from earthly to heavenly. Translated by their Lord into a new world of righteousness and purity and truth, of fellowship with Him and through Him with the Father, that was indeed a kingdom to them ; a kingdom which should one day immeasurably transcend even in outward splendour all the kingdoms of the earth ; but for the outward glories of which they were content to wait. Not so he. The kingdom of One who had not where to lay his head, who was not ministered unto, but laboriously ministered to others, whom the princes of this world rejected and despised, that was no kingdom to him ; and he felt it a fraud and a wrong that he should ever have been inveigled into it ; and thus there may have grown up in him the resolve so to separate and extricate himself from it, as to mark his sense of this wrong. But of this presently something more.

But what shall we say to the admission by the Lord of such a man into the innermost fellowship of his chosen ? We shall best, I think, say that Love 'hopeth all things ; ' and

He who was incarnate Love may well have hoped that, in nearest communion with Himself, the perilous elements in the life of one who, gained for his kingdom, would probably have been a mighty gain, might very possibly be overcome and cast out; for the kingdom of grace is a kingdom not of necessity, but of freedom. And if any make a difficulty here, that so, by this choice of Christ, the guilt of Judas was infinitely exaggerated and enhanced, became far greater than otherwise it would have been, we shall not deny the difficulty, but only urge in reply, What is this, after all, but the same moral difficulty which meets us everywhere? Why should great opportunities be afforded to any, which they misuse, deepening their condemnation thereby; nay, why is any talent committed to any man, which he does not lay out for God, but elects rather to squander or to hide? It is not that we are not here face to face with a mystery, but that it is one repeating itself in the case of every living soul which has ever received, or shall receive, the grace of God in vain.

Let me say the same in respect of a more tremendous mystery still. Who is there that, in thoughtful moments, has not stood almost in a shuddering awe at the fact, that the bag should have been committed to Judas, as it were to evoke and provoke his sin, that sin to which he was tempted the most, and to give him an easy opportunity of indulging it? And yet will any deny that this, too, is only one example more of that which is evermore recurring in that mysterious world in which our lives are being lived? Is it not true that men continually find themselves in conditions especially calculated to call out the master sin of their hearts? Not, indeed, that this is altogether inexplicable, if only we will realize the fact, that these conditions are probably the only ones which would enable them to overcome that sin; that victories can only be won at the hazard of defeats; that great gains cannot be made in the kingdom of

heaven more than anywhere else, except at
the risk of corresponding losses ; and, more-
over, that the sin which a temptation elicits
was already existing; that all which the
temptation did was to gather to a head, and
to bring into evidence, a sickness before dif-
fused through the whole moral frame.

If this answer does not perfectly satisfy, if
much still remains obscure in this, as in so
many other dealings of God with men, all
which faith can do here is to take God upon
trust ; for the sake of that which we *can* understand about Him and his righteousness and
mercy and truth, to trust Him for that which
we cannot understand; reverently keeping
silence before Him, whose judgments are a
great deep, whose throne is encompassed
round with clouds and with darkness; and
then, seeing that these things are so, to pray
with an ever stronger earnestness, ' Lord, lead
us not into temptation ; or, if Thou leadest,
if there is a needs be that the temptation
should come, if only so we can be revealed to

ourselves, see our sin and so grapple with
and overcome it, make Thou *with* the temptation a way of escape from it. If we must
needs walk through fires, do Thou cause, for
Thou only canst, that they shall not kindle
upon us.'

And on this matter of temptation, have we
not much more to learn from the fall of this
apostle?

Occasional and fragmentary as are the
glimpses which we obtain of him, we cannot
trace him step by step, as he treads the downward path, with the same exactness with which
it is possible to trace some others. And yet
of some things we may be sure. Not all at
once, we may be quite certain, did that last
hideous sin take shape in his mind. Little
by little he must have given place to the sug-
gestions of the Evil One, until, in the end,
that Evil One entered into him, and possessed
him wholly. Had he been told at the first
what he should do at the last, his, no doubt,
would have been something of the indignant

reply of the Syrian captain to Elisha, when
the prophet announced to him that he should
murder his master: 'Is thy servant a dog
that he should do this?'[1] There was perhaps,
at first, in this apostle a resentful displeasure,
as I suggested just now, that he should have
been entangled through false and flattering
hopes in that fellowship of reproach and
poverty and pain. Where was the kingdom
of which the Master spake? Where the
thrones on which his chosen servants should
sit, and share with Him in that kingdom and
its glory? How unlike the fulfilment to the
promise! And then there may have grown
up within him, little by little, a determination
to revenge himself, to show that he was not
one who could with impunity be deceived.
And so a passing discontent and disappoint-
ment ripened into deadliest hate; and in
what sin that hate uttered itself at last we all
know too well.

Stand in awe, dear brethren, of many things,

[1] 2 Kings viii. 13.

but of nothing stand more in awe than of
your own selves, and of the dread potential-
ities of evil, no less than of good, which you
bear about with you. Believe me, there is no
smallest spark from Satan's stithy, which, if
duly fanned, or even if left unquenched
and not trodden out, might not increase into
a flame, which should set on fire in you the
whole course of nature; even as in this ma-
terial world there is in each tiniest spark a
possible conflagration, such as should wrap
whole forests or whole cities in flame. Resist
evil at the beginning. Then it is weak and
you are strong; but, after a little allowance,
the conditions will be reversed, and you will
be weak and it strong. Blessed is he who
taketh these little ones of Babylon, and
dasheth them against the stones of God's
law. Stand in awe, I would say again, of
your own selves. He knows very little of
himself who does not know that, as there is a
possible heaven, so there is a possible hell
within him. In the passing thought of im-

purity there is that which, being admitted,
indulged, cherished, followed up whither it
seeks to lead, would mould us, at last, into
the hideous likeness of a Tiberius, or a Louis
the Fifteenth. In the smallest act, word, or
thought of genuine malice, there is shut up a
whole world of cruelty, of intensest delight in
the sufferings of others, such as a Domitian or
an Eccelino never have surpassed.

Thus *he* found it, who probably began with
no more than that passing resentment at his
fancied wrongs, but who, brooding over these,
fell from one wickedness to another, until at
length he had consummated that deed of the
most treacherous wrong which the world has
ever seen. And yet, who will dare to affirm
that even then—even after that sin had been
completed—all had irrecoverably gone from
him? Who will dare to affirm that there was
not even for him a possible place for repentance, though he never found it? Ah, brethren,
if only there had been aught in him which at
all resembled the tears of St. Peter—he, too,

though he had not betrayed, yet having not
only deserted, but with oaths denied his Lord
—if there had been tears such as Peter shed,
when Christ looked at him, and he, at that
look, went out and wept bitterly! And yet,
how could such have been here? They only
flow from the contemplation of forgiving love;
and to believe in that forgiving love, how
impossible it is for the unloving, how hard it
is for us all; projecting, as we do, from our
own hearts a God like to ourselves, and then
cowering before, or fleeing from, the dark
image which we ourselves have created. It
was exactly this, namely, to believe in that
forgiving love, which the betrayer could not
do; else he too might have found pardon in
that very blood which mainly through his
treason had been shed.

Remorse this man could feel, but not repentance; yet, oh! the difference that there is
between these; remorse, of the earth earthly,
of the flesh fleshly; and if I should add, of
the devil devilish, I should scarcely say too

much ; born as it is, not of grief to have offended a loving Father, and done despite to a
gracious Spirit, but of wounded pride, of anger
against ourselves, that the proud idol of self,
worshipped till now, lies by our own act
shattered in the dust, and cannot be worshipped any more. Remorse, if it have tears at
all, they are tears scorching, withering, drying
up with their fierce heat every green thing in
the soul. But the tears of repentance, when
the hard rock of some sinner's heart has been
smitten by Christ's cross as by a rod, and
these waters gush freely forth, how different
an operation is theirs, healing, quickening,
and reviving wheresoever they come. Remorse, it is that ' sorrow of the world ' whereof
the apostle speaks, as a sorrow which ' worketh
death,'[1] which literally worked death in him,
of whom this day we have been speaking,
his end furnishing a dreadful commentary on
that statement of St. Paul's.

A few words on that end of his. He, the

---

[1] 2 Cor. vii. 10.

Ahitophel of the New Covenant, and this at
once in his sin—for they were alike traitors—
and in his self-inflicted doom—for they were
alike self-murderers—as he was not the first,
so was he very far from the last of those who,
finding the knot of their life inextricably
tangled, have counted in a wild despair that
nothing remained but to cut it, and who thus
with profane hand have broken into the
bloody house of their own life; even as the
scorpion—for so men once believed—which,
being girdled with fire, seeks through its own
sting a sort of deliverance from the flames
which encompass it. As he was not the first,
as little was he the last of these; while the
number, I believe, of those who have trod
upon the verge of this sin, who, in utter loathing of a life emptied by their own act of all
its glory and its grace, have longed exceed-
ingly to find a grave, and been almost tempted
guiltily to seek one for themselves, though
of God's restraining mercy kept back from
this crowning guilt, the number of these is

numberless. So terrible a thing is the conscience of sin, when once it is seen as sin, but
has not yet been seen as sin atoned for and
put away; so clinging a curse is it felt—to
be likened to nothing so well as to that robe
of poison and fire which the fabled hero of
antiquity, having in an evil hour put on,
sought in vain to tear away, until in the intolerable anguish of it, death seemed to him
better than life, than such a long agony as
life for him had become.

May God grant that for us, my brethren,
the knowledge of sin may ever go hand-in-
hand with the knowledge of One who has
borne that sin, and so borne it that He has
borne it away for ever. For when once the
arrow of the Almighty has pierced us, there
are no charmed words, no medicines which
the earth affords, potent enough to cause that
barbed arrow to drop from our side. Wheresoever the wounded one turns, he whom God has
wounded, in solitudes or in crowds, in the desert
or the city, at his up-rising and down-lying,

that arrow clings to him still; and there is but One physician, the same who wounded, that can also heal; there is but One who has the sovereign dittany, at whose prevailing touch the arrow that drunk up the spirit, and poisoned the very springs of the life, comes away, and the man is whole once more. Seek we to Him, else for one or another of us that guiltiest day may arrive, as it arrived for the unhappy apostle, when death shall seem rather to be chosen than life, when the dark secrets of death shall seem less dreadful than the intolerable anguish of a sin-burdened life.

And thus, brethren beloved, I bring these discourses, in all likelihood the last which I shall deliver in this place and presence, to a close. I might have chosen some theme lighted up with a more cheerful light, having more of joy and gladness about it; the triumphant lives, for example, of some who were faithful to the end, who let no man take their crown, and who abide for us that come after, as the pillar fires of that desert through which we go, as the shining spires of that Heavenly City toward which we travel. I might have chosen those; but these too, the sadder and sterner and more sombre histories, are not amiss, that from time to time we should meditate on them. And as years grow upon us, there grows also a sense of the tremendous solemnity of life, of that life which we can live but once; and with this there grows further a yearning desire, that if there be any brought within the sphere of our teaching who are living at random, squandering that substance beside which all other treasures are merest dross, to awake in them a consciousness of the same. Let there be any such prodigals of their heavenly substance with us this day, and what has been spoken about others, it surely touches also them. The prophet and the king of the Old Covenant, and, greater than either of these, the apostle of the New, what was there, after all, of more solemn meaning in their lives than in yours,

that the shipwreck of yours should not be as
far-reaching a catastrophe as was ever the
shipwreck of theirs? As set beside two of
these, even had they been faithful to their
trust, you have Christ's assurance that the
least in the kingdom of heaven, in the Church
of Christ, is greater than they, greater in the
dignity to which he is called, but greater
therefore also in the doom wherein he may
be entangled. Gifts specially their own, for
their own special work, they may have received ; but the grace of that day of Pentecost
which they never saw, a grace whereof you
are partakers, is more and mightier than
every gift of theirs.   I invited you to stand in
awe just now of the possibilities of evil which
are in you ; but stand not less in awe of the
possibilities of good, and of the reserves of
glory which may be yours. If there be that
in you which is akin to a dark world of lust,
and hate, and pride around you and beneath
you, if that which would ever persuade you to
lose yourselves in it, there is also that which

is akin to a world of light, and love, and purity, this world also being around you and above. And there is One, the Father of your spirits, the God and Father of our Lord Jesus Christ, who is ever seeking to draw you upward into that higher world, into that kingdom of heaven, which Christ has brought down to earth, that so even in this present time we might find ourselves and our true life there, and that good thing which has been committed to us might at once keep and multiply by the Holy Ghost which has been given us.

LONDON

PRINTED BY SPOTTISWOODE AND CO.

NEW-STREET SQUARE

Books by the same Author.

STUDIES in the GOSPELS.
Demy 8vo. 10s. 6d.

NOTES on the PARABLES of our LORD.
Tenth Edition, carefully revised. 8vo. 12s.

NOTES on the MIRACLES of our LORD.
Eighth Edition, carefully revised. 8vo. 12s.

SYNONYMS of the NEW TESTAMENT.
New Edition. One vol. 8vo. 10s. 6d.

PROVERBS and their LESSONS.
Fifth Edition. Fcp. 8vo. 3s.

SERMONS PREACHED in WESTMINSTER
ABBEY.
Second Edition. 8vo. 10s. 6d.

The FITNESS of HOLY SCRIPTURE for UN-
FOLDING the SPIRITUAL LIFE of MAN: CHRIST th
DESIRE of all NATIONS; or, The UNCONSCIOUS PRO
PHECIES of HEATHENDOM.
Hulsean Lectures. Fourth Edition. Fcp. 8vo. 5s.

On the AUTHORIZED VERSION of the NEW
TESTAMENT.
Second Edition. 8vo. 7s.

COMMENTARY on the EPISTLES to the
SEVEN CHURCHES in ASIA.
Third Edition. 8vo. 8s. 6d.

SACRED LATIN POETRY.
Chiefly Lyrical. Selected and arranged for Use. Second Edition,
corrected and improved. Fcp. 8vo. 7s.

Books by the same Author.

POEMS.
Collected and arranged anew.   Fcp. 8vo. 7s. 6d.

JUSTIN MARTYR and other POEMS.
Fifth Edition.   Fcp. 8vo. 6s.

ELEGIAC POEMS.
Third Edition.   Fcp. 8vo. 2s. 6d.

CALDERON'S LIFE'S a DREAM : The GREAT THEATRE of the World.
With an Essay on his Life and Genius.   Fcp. 8vo. 4s. 6d.

GUSTAVUS ADOLPHUS : SOCIAL ASPECTS of the THIRTY YEARS' WAR.
Two Lectures.   Fcp. 8vo. 2s. 6d.

ENGLISH PAST and PRESENT.
Fifth Edition.   Fcp. 8vo. 4s.

SELECT GLOSSARY of ENGLISH WORDS
Used formerly in Senses different from the Present.   Third Edition. Fcp. 8vo. 4s.

On SOME DEFICIENCIES in our ENGLISH DICTIONARIES.
Second Edition.   8vo. 3s.

On the STUDY of WORDS.
Twelfth Edition, carefully revised.   Fcp. 8vo. 4s.

MACMILLAN and CO. London.

Recent Publications.

Works by Dr. J. B. Lightfoot.

ST. PAUL'S EPISTLE to the GALATIANS.
A Revised Text, with Introduction, Notes, and Dissertations. By J. B. Lightfoot, D.D., Hulsean Professor of Divinity, Cambridge. Second Edition, revised, 8vo. 12s.

ST. PAUL'S EPISTLE to the PHILIPPIANS.
A Revised Text, with Notes and Dissertations. [*In the press.*

Works by Rev. B. F. Westcott, B.D.

AN INTRODUCTION to the STUDY of the FOUR GOSPELS.
By the Rev. B. F. Westcott, B.D. New and Revised Edition, crown 8vo. 10s. 6d.

A HISTORY of the CANON of the NEW TESTAMENT during the FIRST FOUR CENTURIES.
Second Edition, revised, crown 8vo. 10s. 6d.

THE BIBLE in the CHURCH.
A Popular Account of the Collection and Reception of the Holy Scriptures in the Christian Churches. Second Edition. 18mo. 4s. 6d.

CHARACTERISTICS of the GOSPEL MIRACLES.
Sermons Preached before the University of Cambridge. With Notes. Crown 8vo. 4s. 6d.

THE GOSPEL of the RESURRECTION :
Thoughts on its Relation to Reason and History. New Edition. Fcp. 8vo. 4s. 6d.

MACMILLAN and CO. London.

Recent Publications.

WORKS BY DR. C. J. VAUGHAN.

THE WHOLESOME WORDS OF JESUS CHRIST. Four Sermons preached before the University of Cambridge. By C. J. VAUGHAN, D.D. Fcp. 8vo. 3s. 6d.

THE CHURCH OF THE FIRST DAYS. Second Edition. 3 vols. Fcp. 8vo. 4s. 6d. each.

LIFE'S WORK AND GOD'S DISCIPLINE. Three Sermons. Fcp. 8vo. 2s. 6d.

LECTURES ON THE 'EPISTLE TO THE PHILIPPIANS. Second Edition. Crown 8vo. 7s. 6d.

LECTURES ON THE REVELATION OF ST. JOHN. Second Edition. 2 vols. crown 8vo. 15s.

MEMORIALS OF HARROW SUNDAYS. A Selection of Sermons preached in Harrow School Chapel. With a View of the Chapel. Fourth Edition. Crown 8vo. 10s. 6d.

ST. PAUL'S EPISTLE TO THE ROMANS. The Greek Text with English Notes. Second Edition. Crown 8vo. 5s.

LESSONS OF LIFE AND GODLINESS. A Selection of Sermons preached in the Parish Church of Doncaster. Third Edition. Fcp. 8vo. 4s. 6d.

WORDS FROM THE GOSPELS. A .Second Selection of Sermons preached in the Parish Church of Doncaster. Second Edition. Fcp. 8vo. 4s. 6d.

WORKS BY PROFESSOR KINGSLEY.

THE WATER OF LIFE, and other Sermons. By the Rev. CHARLES KINGSLEY, M.A., Rector of Eversley, Professor of Modern History in the University of Cambridge, and Chaplain to the Queen and the Prince of Wales. Fcp. 8vo. 6s.

GOOD NEWS OF GOD. Fourth Edition. Fcp. 8vo. 4s. 6d.

SERMONS FOR THE TIMES. Third Edition. Fcp. 8vo. 3s. 6d.

SERMONS ON NATIONAL SUBJECTS. First Series. Second Edition. Fcp. 8vo. 5s.

SERMONS ON NATIONAL SUBJECTS. Second Series. Second Edition. Fcp. 8vo. 5s.

THE GOSPEL OF THE PENTATEUCH. Second Edition. Fcp. 8vo. 4s. 6d.

DAVID.—Four Sermons :—David's Weakness—David's Strength—David's Anger—David's Deserts. Fcp. 8vo. cloth, 2s. 6d.

VILLAGE SERMONS. Seventh Edition. Fcp. 8vo. 2s. 6d.

MACMILLAN and CO. London.

www.ingramcontent.com/pod-product-compliance
Lightning Source LLC
Chambersburg PA
CBHW021412090426
42742CB00009B/1108